businesspartners

successful
**project
management**

Withdrawn
From Stock

For further success in all aspects of business, be sure to read these other businesspartners books:

Successful Interviews
Successful Coaching & Mentoring
Successful Time Management

businesspartners

successful
project
management

Ken Lawson, M.A., Ed.M.

NEW
HOLLAND

This edition first published in 2009 by New Holland Publishers (UK) Ltd
London • Cape Town • Sydney • Auckland
www.newhollandpublishers.com

Garfield House, 86–88 Edgware Road, London W2 2EA, United Kingdom
80 McKenzie Street, Cape Town 8001, South Africa
Unit 1, 66 Gibbes Street, Chatswood, NSW 2067, Australia
218 Lake Road, Northcote, Auckland, New Zealand

10 8 6 4 2 1 3 5 7 9

© 2005 Axis Publishing Limited
8c Accommodation Road
London NW11 8ED
www.axispublishing.co.uk

NOTE: The opinions and advice expressed in this book are intended as a guide only. The
publisher and author accept no responsibility for any loss sustained as a result of using this
book.

ISBN: 978-1-84773-396-2

Printed and bound in Korea

contents

Introduction

In today's competitive, pressure-packed business world, there's no stronger imperative than to 'get things done' – many things, and in increasingly limited amounts of time. For many managers, the daily challenge is meeting the goals and managing the projects that seem to rise in direct proportion to the fall-off of available time. How can managers defend against and conquer the onslaught of projects that advances more ruthlessly with each passing day? One way is to resolve to work smarter, not harder. *Successful Project Management* is written to enable managers to do just that.

With a clear, methodical approach that models its key recommendations, *Successful Project Management* shows managers how to conceive, plan, implement, monitor and complete the complex projects that are today's pressing workplace priorities. Each of the chapters simplifies the how-tos and whys of effective project management, and provides useful guidelines in concise, easy-to-read text.

The opening chapter explains the importance of clearly defining a project vision and of outlining its objectives and limitations. You'll learn why some managers avoid the planning process, and why that's a strategic error. Chapter 2 details the benefits of thorough planning, and offers proven techniques for creating a project plan and establishing milestones to monitor its progress.

In Chapter 3, you'll develop an understanding of how to estimate the expenditures of time, finances and resources that are key dimensions of every project. Obstacles to effective estimates are clearly defined, and sources of effective estimates are presented alongside tips for setting timelines and defining costs.

No project can proceed effectively without the involvement of a committed, talented project team. *Successful Project Management* explains the manager's role, and why it's critical. You'll learn about different styles of leadership so that you can decide which one may be right for you. The various team roles of participants are clearly described, along with guidelines for appointing members and fostering teamwork. You'll gain new insight on delegating effectively and motivating your team to action.

Managing a project effectively is not an event, but a process. *Successful Project Management* shows you how to get a project off the ground, manage the inevitable uncertainties that crop up along the way, organize information and communicate effectively about it. You'll learn how to monitor each project effectively, provide progress reports, hold review meetings and keep to schedules. You'll also learn how to control costs, avoid unwanted expansion boundaries and manage the risk of veering off course.

A crucial phase in the effective management of any project is the close-down, or conclusion. As the book closes, you'll develop an understanding of the benefits of a thorough plan for closing each project, how to create one and how to allocate resources for it. There are many tips for managing an effective close-down, leading a project review meeting and developing a concluding report that summarizes the project and details its success. There are also tips on celebrating the project's success and thanking the team members.

Managing a project effectively is partly art, partly science. *Successful Project Management* is written to help you plan, manage and succeed in the process. It provides a wealth of effective guidelines and strategies that will help you to rise to the occasion of each new project and conquer it not by working longer hours, but by working smarter.

Ken Lawson, M.A., Ed.M.

Career management counsellor and author

Instructor, School of Continuing and Professional Studies

New York University

1

defining the project

What distinguishes a project?

Project management describes the process taken to ensure the success of a particular project. It is distinguished by:

1 A PARTICULAR GOAL

A project has a clear objective and target, unlike routine, everyday activities such as answering the phone or responding to e-mails that are simply a means to an end. For instance, statements such as 'to double sales within six months' or 'to build a new office block within two years' demand a particular course of action that may deviate from a company's habitual way of running business. Identifying an established goal means it is easy to quantify whether the project has succeeded or not.

2 TIME BOUNDARIES

A project has a specific start and end date, another characteristic that distinguishes it from a routine activity that is part of a process that has no defined completion date.

3 A TOOL FOR CHANGE
A project aims to shake up the status quo or to respond to external change. In both cases, an effective project will have an easily identifiable (and sometimes irreversible) impact.

4 SPECIFIC RESOURCES
Setting up a project demands the allocation of a particular time period and a chosen group of people to work on the project with a specified amount of money and resources including information, equipment and facilities.

5 AN ELEMENT OF RISK
A project involves a new way of approaching things. This constitutes an element of risk, no matter how carefully the plan of action has been considered. It is fraught with uncertainties because the project can't rely on an already successful template. For instance, a project usually builds a new team of people who haven't worked together before, causing potential friction.

Project benefits

These are some of the many advantages that the tools and techniques of project management can bring to managers and their organizations.

1 ENCOURAGES GREATER FOCUS ON KEY GOALS
Setting up a project encourages you to concentrate on what is really important for your company. It forces you to set priorities, thus spending less time and energy on less consequential parts of the business that may be preventing you from achieving your main goals.

2 CREATES URGENCY
A project by nature has a specific time span – whether it's six weeks or six months. Therefore, you and your team can measure exactly what you have achieved or what is left to be done by a specific deadline. Companies often thrive from the intensity and pressure created by a clearly defined time frame.

3 HELPS ADAPT TO CHANGE
In today's increasingly unpredictable marketplace new trends
and developments emerge very rapidly and companies will
only survive if they are quick to change. Projects provide a
framework to analyze these shifts and to prepare a response
that will then create more change.

4 SAVES MONEY
Many companies find they are putting a lot of investment
into different areas but are not achieving desired results.
This is often down to poor planning. The discipline required
for running a project encourages a tight rein on budgets.

5 INCREASES CONTROL

If you underestimate the importance of a well-thought-out plan, you can find yourself reacting too late to a change in the market or to an aggressive move by a competitor. However, if you devote time to meticulously planning a project, you will feel far more proactive. By forcing yourself to create a template for action, you and your company will be buoyed by a clear sense of direction.

6 MINIMIZES RISKS
Potential pitfalls are always lurking in business, but if you and your company have created a carefully considered plan of action, you will have factored in all the possible threats as well as made some contingency plans to lessen any negative effects.

7 MAXIMIZES RESULTS
Spending a lot of time on activities will not always translate into the desired results. Effective planning helps you to achieve the maximum result from a given effort.

defining the project

Why bypass planning?

It's useful to identify why many managers mistakenly bypass the planning stages. This way, you can avoid repeating their mistakes:

COMPANY CULTURE

1 COST/FINANCIAL RESTRAINTS
Less forward-thinking companies are eager to push projects ahead in order to see quick results. Managers feel forced to be seen to be doing something and are discouraged from spending time mapping out a plan. In these companies, time spent planning is also regarded as a waste of money, since there are no immediate benefits.

2 FIRE-FIGHTING MENTALITY
When companies are involved in several activities or projects at the same time and managers are involved in managing a series of small crises, the senior management simply think there is no time for more strategic planning.

3 OVER-RELIANCE ON CONSULTANTS
With so many managers involved in resolving small problems,
companies often rely on external consultants to analyze some
of the company's structural problems. An outsider's view of a
business can sometimes be healthy and insightful, but too
much dependence on consultants means the company's own
managers are unable to assess situations they are closer to on
a daily basis.

INDIVIDUAL RELUCTANCE

1 LAZINESS
People are naturally more inclined to stick to old and tried methods, even if they are not working.

2 RISK AVERSION
Many managers are reluctant to stick out their necks to implement changes that might fail, so they shy away from adopting new approaches to an old problem.

3 OVERCONFIDENCE

The longer that managers have been working in a company, the more they have learned to rely on their own experience to resolve both new and ongoing issues. Even if problems persist, they can deceive themselves that their working methods are the best.

4 POOR EXPERIENCE

Once a manager has been involved in a project that was badly conceived, they will be less open to launching their own projects, particularly if the company culture doesn't encourage forward planning.

defining the project

The project objective

It is imperative to have a firm and concise agreement as to what a project should attempt to achieve before starting any plan. Without a clear definition, a project is virtually doomed to failure from the outset. Because of its importance, it's not unusual for the definition phase to take the longest amount of time in the project management process.

WHO HAD THE IDEA FIRST?

All projects emerge from a pressing need to change or to create something new (for instance, to acquire a competitor, to launch a new product or to expand overseas).

As a preliminary step, it is useful for the project manager – who will be in charge of planning and implementing the project – to try to track down the person or people, inside or outside the company, who formulated the need or the idea initially.

THE FOLLOWING ARE THE MOST COMMON ORIGINATORS OF IDEAS:

1 CUSTOMERS

Clients are often the main drivers for change. For instance, take the case of a supplier of men's casual attire. The company is asked by one of its biggest clients, a department store, whether it has considered branching out into sports leisure wear, which they have identified as the fastest growing market within the casual attire sector.

For the supplier, a new clothing line will entail significant investment in their factories as well as changes in the way they operate. Maybe some of their traditional clothing lines will be affected. Therefore, it's crucial to go back to the client and find out exactly what percentage of future business they believe that sports leisure is likely to represent.

If the client can make a persuasive argument, the company may decide, after a close study of the market and by talking to other clients, that a move into sports clothing is indeed a viable project.

2 CONSULTANTS

Consultancies can also recommend major changes to companies, particularly if they have been expressly hired to identify new business opportunities.

Imagine the clothing supplier has hired a consultant to analyze the company. If a report comes back recommending that the supplier diversify into sports leisure clothing, the project manager should evaluate the viability of the findings by gauging their main clients' interest in new clothing lines.

3 SENIOR MANAGEMENT
A senior director at the clothing supplier may have suggested
that a foray into a new sports clothing line is the way forwards
to combat dwindling sales in the men's casual attire market.
But the director is only acting on a hunch – and hasn't made a
proper analysis to back the suggestion up – another colleague,
the potential project manager, is expected to evaluate the
idea. This senior manager can also be referred to as a sponsor
or a project champion.

4 PROJECT MANAGER
The idea to diversify may have come from you. In this case, the
onus to sell the project idea to others is on you. The individuals
who will be interested in the project, also commonly known
as stakeholders, will include clients, customers, senior
management, contractors, suppliers, the accounts department
and even consultants.

HOW MUCH SUPPORT IS THERE?

Now that you've established who expressed the original idea, you need to find out how much support the idea has. Basically, you need to ask whether the project is feasible and whether other members of the company agree. Here are some steps to follow that will help you to decide.

1 GATHER MANAGEMENT AND CLIENT OPINIONS
At this stage, seek feedback from as many different sources as possible. If a client is pushing the project, check first with senior management to see if they are interested. If they reject the idea outright, there is little point in hearing views from colleagues with less influence on a final decision. If senior management is enthusiastic about the idea, check with all your clients.

2 FIND DEVIL'S ADVOCATES

Deliberately approach the most negative people in the company, especially if you are keen on the project. Fault finders and nit-pickers are very useful as devil's advocates and for underlining all the potential pitfalls in a project. Make sure you don't reveal your bias when you mention the idea. Try to be as neutral as possible so people you ask don't feel they are being swayed one way or another.

3 PUT THE PROJECT INTO CONTEXT

Particularly in the case of larger companies, there could be several projects on the go. It's important to find out about all existing and potential projects and to gauge how the new project fits in. Putting your project into a broader context is a test about how urgent and significant your particular project is. Ask yourself the following questions:

- Does your project seem less urgent? How does it fit in with the organization's long-term goals?
- How much overall funding exists for new ventures? Have all necessary funds already been allocated to another project?
- Is the timing right? Can your project wait? Does it matter if your project is postponed? Could other competing projects be shelved?

4 WEIGH THE PROS AND CONS

By this stage, you will have gathered a comprehensive list of the driving versus the resisting forces (pros and cons). It is useful to grade the different forces out of ten and see which side scores higher. If there is no obvious winner – the advantages and disadvantages cancel each other out – you may want to go back to your different sources and ask them to grade the pros and cons in case you've overlooked the value of any of the competing forces.

DEFINING THE VISION

Assuming you've decided that the original idea has the potential and feasibility to become a major project, now is the time to come up with an overall statement that summarizes the vision of the project. These are suggested steps to take:

1 DEFINE KEY PLAYERS

Whereas in your initial information-gathering process, you were trying to get as varied and eclectic a number of opinions as possible, you should now be narrowing the list of participants to those people who are going to play a central role in the project.

Key players will include the project manager, the sponsor or most senior member in the company who is ultimately responsible for giving the project the green light, the client (or the person or people who are going to most directly benefit from the project) and potential colleagues who will make up the company team working on the project.

2 GET FEEDBACK

Ask the key players to write down their opinions on:

■ What the company wants to change and how.

■ Why they think the project is important.

■ What the project will achieve.

■ How soon it should be implemented.

At this stage, it is preferable not to arrange a meeting with all participants – this approach will allow all players to voice their true opinions and intents without being unduly influenced by others.

3 SPELL OUT A VISION STATEMENT
After you've considered and amalgamated the different
opinions of the key players, you are closer to formulating the
project's vision or mission statement.

Keep the statement as free from technical jargon as possible,
and make it brief (no longer than one or two sentences) as
this guarantees a clear, unambiguous statement that everyone
can understand. For instance, in the case of the supplier of
men's casual attire, the statement would read: 'The company
seeks to diversify into the growing sportswear market to
create new business and to overcome falling sales in
traditional men's casual wear'.

4 ARRANGE A MEETING
Set up a meeting with all key players and show them the
vision statement. Allow all participants to air their opinions on
the statement to see that it encompasses most of the players'
objectives. Only if most participants are in agreement can you
guarantee continued commitment to the project.

Setting objectives

When all participants have agreed on a general vision of the project, it is time to set objectives that will help to make the vision a reality.

WHY SETTING OBJECTIVES IS IMPORTANT

1 TARGETS
Set targets can spur the company into action by motivating team members.

2 SENSE OF PURPOSE
Objectives create a sense of direction as they focus on achieving goals.

3 PRIORITIZATION
Objectives force the team to prioritize and organize work.

THE ESSENTIAL CHARACTERISTICS OF OBJECTIVES

1 SPECIFIC

It is important that the objective is clear and simple. For the clothing supplier to state that it 'wants to increase sales' is too vague. It is better to state the main intent: 'the company aims to gain an x per cent of the sport leisure market within 18 months that will represent x per cent of overall revenue'.

2 MEASURABLE

It is vital that you are able to measure the objective's success, whether within eight weeks or eight months. For that, you have to have a list of indicators, for instance, comparing sales figures for the new sports line for the first three months with sales figures for the same quarter a year later.

3 AGGRESSIVE
Setting up a project is in itself an aggressive move because it is a positive action to achieve a desired effect. It is fitting that the targets should be ambitious.

4 REALISTIC
It is no use for a clothing supplier, for instance, to aim to become the main supplier of sports wear for three department stores within a year. This is too huge a leap from its current businessmen's casual attire. The targets should be appropriate to the investment available, the overall market scenario, including the action taken by competitors and the capabilities of the staff. Unrealistic goals will demotivate staff.

5 TIME-SENSITIVE
A cut-off point to measure what has been achieved so far and how much is left to accomplish creates urgency.

POINTS TO REMEMBER

1 PRIORITIZE
A company is likely to have several objectives. List them in order of importance.

2 GET BACKING
A majority of key players should agree with the objectives.

3 BE ADAPTABLE
Objectives may change as the project develops. Don't worry if new targets have to be set. When creating a new list of objectives, go through the same process of defining them.

Setting limitations

The objectives are generally the desired results of the company. However, you have to be ready to challenge the inevitable list of limitations and constraints facing any project. The most common limitations are:

1 TIME CONSTRAINTS

It's inevitable that clients and senior management, because of the pressures they are both facing, will impose a time frame that is much shorter than the project team envisages. In many scenarios, the two sides will negotiate a time frame that is more or less satisfactory for both.

It's important to identify who is setting the time limit and how much scope there is for shifting the time frames. Does the market require delivery, for instance, by Christmas, or is management or the client imposing a deadline because it prefers to be ahead of schedule? Whatever option, you need to know.

2 BUDGET CONSTRAINTS
In the same way, customers and senior management are looking at the bottom line and pushing for the lowest budget possible. The project team, however, is intent on delivering a quality product and is more interested in procuring the best talent and equipment for the project. Both sides may have unrealistic expectations.

As project manager, you will have to find out as much as possible about the resources of the project sponsor or client and change your expectations and the requirements of the project accordingly.

3 STRUCTURAL CONSTRAINTS

Your project plan may have the approval of the senior management but is viewed with less enthusiasm by a separate division of the company. This division may object to some of the goals and may have enough clout or bargaining power to set limits on some of your smaller targets.

Trade unions may also view the changes potentially created by your project as a threat to jobs or working practices. You have to take into account the opinions of people in the company who are not embracing the project, and you may have to make some compromises.

4 RISKS

There are many potential external factors beyond your control, for instance, a plunging stock market, an unexpected buyout of the company or a dramatic fall in consumer spending, which you should always factor into your objectives.

The desire for success can make companies blind to many of the potential pitfalls. You need to bear in mind all these possibilities and also calculate how likely they are to happen. Try, for instance, looking at sales growth not only from the point of view of your company but on the basis of new competitors entering the market, or of a well-known local company venturing into the sector.

Once you've implemented some measures to minimize potential threats, it's a good idea to review all of them and to identify any new risks. If you've already been through the usual possibilities, try role playing to work through the various possibilities, successes and failures.

42

defining the project

Checklist: project definition

1 Have you spoken to the person (or people) who had the idea for the project in the first place? ☐

2 Has that person (or people) expressed the idea succinctly? ☐

3 If it was your idea, have you communicated it clearly to other team members? ☐

4 Does the project have a sponsor? ☐

5 If you have been appointed project manager, are you confident that you have the firm backing of a senior executive who will support you if things get difficult? ☐

6 Is there a general consensus among key players about the project's main vision? ☐

7 Can you think of other company goals that may take priority over your project? ☐

8 Would the project suffer if it was postponed? ☐

CHECKLIST

9 How much would delaying the project affect the company? ☐

10 Have you identified the fundamental issues that must be addressed before you are convinced that the project is viable? ☐

11 Can you list one to three main objectives of the project in a sentence each? ☐

12 Are the objectives measurable? ☐

13 What indicators are you using to measure objectives? ☐

14 Is there a specific time frame to the project? Is it realistic? ☐

15 Have you and the company understood the risks involved in undertaking the project? ☐

16 Have you thought of any contingency plans? ☐

CHECKLIST

2

planning the project

planning the project
The benefits of a plan

PRELIMINARY PLANNING
Once you've defined your objectives, you are clear about why you are embarking on the project. Now you need to know how you are going to reach your objective. The next step is to make a plan.

WHAT IS A PLAN?
It is a detailed account or proposal of how something can be done or achieved. In project management terms, it signals that you and your company have an outline or map that you intend to follow to ensure that you reach your objectives.

This section focuses on the preliminary planning stages of the project. The more detailed planning of budgets and schedules and creation of the project teams are discussed in Chapter 3, pp 64-95. The following shows how a plan can work to your company's benefit:

1

LOOKS AT THE BIGGER PICTURE
A plan forces the project manager to think about the company's main priorities, as well as the use of available resources, the budget, the project schedule and how many team members to recruit.

2 SETS A REFERENCE POINT
If there is a template that the project manager and team can constantly refer to, it is easier to track developments or spot any improvized action that veers away from what was agreed. It is particularly valuable to diffuse arguments because it serves as a reference point for everyone involved.

3 COMMUNICATES A VISION
A plan can serve as a very effective communications tool. A well-presented and succinctly written plan can be sent out to all the main players, including customers, team members, suppliers, sponsors and stakeholders.

4 DELEGATES TASKS
A plan helps the project manager to list all the separate tasks and assignments that have to be covered and makes delegation much easier. It will ensure that everyone has a defined role.

5 IS EASY TO PARTITION
Although it's essential for the project manager to have a master plan, for the different players it's sometimes clearer if they can follow a smaller part of the plan that affects them directly. This ensures they can meet their goals.

6 ALLOWS INCREASED CONTROL
Often, there will be one master plan for the project that covers everything that needs to happen. The project manager is likely to show the different players only the parts of the plan that are relevant to them.

7 SETS CLEAR ROLES

A plan avoids confusion about who does what and what must be delivered or completed when. People have fewer excuses for missing deadlines.

8 ADAPTS TO CHANGE

Finally, although plans ease efficiency and create direction, they are not etched in stone. If during the implementation of the project, new developments emerge that change the original assumptions the plan was based on, don't be afraid to alter the plan. But make sure that everyone is in agreement with the changes, that they are kept informed and that they stick to the new plan.

Creating a plan

These are the recommended steps for creating a preliminary action plan, starting with researching previous case histories and brainstorming ideas with key players to creating an ordered list of core tasks for your project, grouped by function:

1

RESEARCH COMPANY HISTORY

Although every project is unique, it is possible that the company has already carried out a similar project in the past. If the project, for instance introducing a new computer system in the company, was successful at the time, it may be useful to refer to any documents of the previous plan.

This doesn't mean that it will still be relevant to the current situation, but it is worth consulting previous templates and talking to any staff members who were involved with similar projects. Thorough research of similar projects undertaken by competitors could also save you invaluable time.

2 PLAN A BRAINSTORMING MEETING
Although, as the project manager, you might already have a
clear idea of what are the most important things to get on
with, it is imperative to keep an open mind at this stage.

Gather all key players of the project together at a meeting and
ask them to come up with activities they think are important
to achieve the project's objectives.

Follow the rules of brainstorming by appointing one member
(preferably not yourself to avoid criticism of bias) to chair the
meeting and to invite members to come up with ideas at
random. Don't criticize or analyze the ideas at this stage.
This is an exploratory stage where people may come up with
activities that you have overlooked. You may be surprised
by the new angles or approaches that people bring to
the meeting.

3 DRAW UP A LIST OF ACTIVITIES
No matter how irrelevant or inconsequential, make sure you
jot down all the activities, effectively tasks or actions, that you
have to carry out to achieve an objective. This list is different
from a simpler 'to do' list in that it focuses on the achievement
of a single goal.

4 REVIEW THE LIST
Towards the end of the meeting, when contributions might
be drying up, go through the list aloud with participants
and start discarding the activities that most people agree
are irrelevant.

5 REORDER THE LIST

Preferably at a separate sitting, when you have had time to digest some of the contributions, you have to start imposing an order on the possibly long list in front of you. Allocate priorities to the task by giving them scores from 1 (unimportant) to 10 (highly important). If too many tasks have a high priority, run through the list again and demote the less important ones. Once you have done this, rewrite the list in priority order.

6 GROUP ACTIVITIES INTO CLUSTERS

It is likely that the list is still too long and that even if you have sorted out which are the most important activities, there is still no logical connection to the sequence. It is useful now to divide the activities into clusters based on functions or departments involved.

7 GROUP CHRONOLOGICALLY
The most effective way to group activities is to consider the order in which they are likely to happen. For instance, if the project involves the launch of a new household product, the research and development process is going to take place at the beginning of the cycle and the details of a TV campaign must be tackled after the product details are ironed out.

8 GROUP BY COST
Advertising and marketing may involve the highest cost in the project, but they will still be a lower priority chronologically. Some activities like funding, which affects all groups, should be left as separate entities that have permanent importance to the project.

9 ARRANGE FURTHER MEETING
Once you have a comprehensive list of activities split into
groups and placed into a logical sequence, show them to all
key players. This allows other people to note any gaping holes
and overlaps or to query the plan's sequence of activities.

10 DRAW UP A FINAL LIST
After inserting new comments and going through the planned
activities to double-check the sequence, put the list aside for a
few days so that you return to it with a fresh perspective.

When you draw up the final list, make sure that the
descriptions of the activities answer the following questions:

■ Is the description clear and concise? Are you sure it would be
   understood by any key player in the project?

■ Does the description state how long the activity will take?

■ Is there any indication of what resources (money, personnel
   and equipment) will be needed to carry out the action?

Creating milestones

Now that you've established a preliminary list of activities, you need to devise a way of monitoring (discussed in greater detail in Chapter 6, pp. 152-209) that the activities are producing the intended results (a term commonly referred to as deliverables).

A common way of doing this is to set milestones, key events or achievements during the project that will indicate that the activities have achieved results. These are some of their benefits and characteristics:

BENEFITS OF MILESTONES

1 MEASURES PROGRESS
Senior directors looking through an initial plan will be reassured that the project manager has included a way of checking that targets are being met. Things that can be quantified make shareholders and sponsors less nervous about the outcome of a project.

2 FOCUSES ON RESULTS
A list of activities can be very long. To address this, milestones create urgency and direction by breaking up periods of work into easily identifiable results. Management is reassured by these, and staff, in turn, are motivated by the steady progress it creates.

3 DIVIDES WORK SCHEDULE
Milestones can provide natural breaks. It is important not to create too many breaks for their own sake as this can pressurize staff to come up with statements of progress at inopportune times.

4 ALERTS TO DIFFICULTIES
If certain actions in the project aren't yielding results, a missed milestone can often inform the project team of any important errors that are occurring within the system.

IDEAL CHARACTERISTICS OF MILESTONES

1
SPACED INTERVALS
Milestones are spaced at intervals of typically every two weeks to a month (although this can often be more frequent in shorter projects).

2
DIRECT STATEMENTS
Milestones should make statements that are clear and direct. For instance, in the case of the clothing supplier that is moving into sports fashion, one milestone would be the 'signing of a new contract with x department store'; another milestone would be the 'first delivery of the sports merchandise to the store'.

3 VERIFIABLE RESULTS

Milestones usually occur when concrete actions take place with definite results so that they are easily verifiable.

4 ADAPTABILITY

Like the plan of activities, a milestone plan should be used only as a useful template or reference point. Project managers don't have to stick slavishly to them. If there are major developments during the project, milestones that are no longer relevant can be shifted or omitted altogether.

Checklist: planning

1 Have you checked if the company has carried out a similar project in the past? Are there any lessons to be learned? ☐

2 Have you taken into account the opinions of everyone involved in the project? Are you sure you haven't overlooked some important activities in the plan? ☐

3 Are all of the activities in your action plan necessary? ☐

4 Do the results of the activities listed genuinely carry out the objectives set out by the company? ☐

5 Would the plan be hampered if you changed the chronological sequence of the activities listed? ☐

6 Have you included details of cost and timing in the descriptions of activities? ☐

7 Was there general approval for the final plan or did you have to spend some time negotiating? ☐

8 Have you remembered to include ways of checking that the activities in the plan are producing the desired results? ☐

9 Have you thought about setting milestones? ☐

CHECKLIST

estimating time,
resources and money

66

estimating time, resources and money

Overview

At this stage, you've established your goals and the benefits of the project, in other words the 'what' and 'why' of the project. You've also begun to map out a draft plan and a possible ordering of activities as well as to look into ways of monitoring whether targets have been reached. The next move is to answer the how-to-achieve-the-project phase more accurately.

THIS CHAPTER LOOKS AT THE THREE BASIC ASPECTS OF PLANNING:

1 HOW MUCH TIME WILL THE PROJECT TAKE?
At this stage, it's more than likely that you don't know how long your project will take to complete. However you need to estimate a rough deadline and compare it with the schedule your client or sponsor is hoping to meet.

2 WHAT RESOURCES DOES THE PROJECT NEED?
Although resources include the often forgotten basics such as computer equipment, stationery, office space and furniture, the most essential components are the workforce. Whatever budget constraints you may be facing, you have to balance these with the pressures of delivering a quality product or service in reasonable time. You can't afford to not appoint the best possible team at your disposal.

3 HOW MUCH WILL THE PROJECT COST?

There's no way of escaping the project manager's most pressing dilemma: clients are pressing to lower costs all the time, while workers demand higher benefits. To best negotiate with both parties, you need to have a firm grip on the direct costs involved (salaries, equipment and travel), indirect costs (ongoing overheads like electricity, stationery, shared receptionists) and the availability of contingency funds so that you're ready for the worst possible case scenario.

Obstacles to effective estimates

There are several reasons why estimating time, resources and money
can go wrong:

1 MISSING ACTIVITIES
The initial list in your project plan (Chapter 2, p. 57) is
incomplete so you don't identify all your tasks until the middle
of the implementation phase. Making time for new activities
eats into the schedule.

2 CHANGING OBJECTIVES
When the goal posts start to shift in the middle of the project,
sometimes due to inadequate definitions in the early phase,
then changes have to be made, and time is lost.

3 OVER-OPTIMISM
When the sponsor or senior management is pushing for a deadline that is convenient for them but unrealistic and you don't challenge the assumptions, you have an optimistic timetable that is doomed to miss its deadline.

4 POOR COMMUNICATION
As the project manager, you have to try to relay information between the suppliers, the team responsible for the tasks and the end users, almost instantly. Otherwise, the opposite ends of a project are working within different parameters.

Sources of estimates

The most common sources of estimates a project manager can refer to in the first instance are:

1 EXPERIENCE

If you've worked on other projects (even of a different size and scope), then you can rely on your personal knowledge of common pitfalls. If you haven't, ask other key players about their experiences.

2 RECORDED DATA

Ideally, your company will have stored files (electronic or hard copy) of past projects that you can refer to for some pointers. A search in the library, or online, of similar projects can also yield some useful case studies.

3 CONSULTANTS
It may be premature to hire external experts for advice when you haven't drawn up a formal budget, but if this is a necessary step that will help you to avoid common mistakes, make sure you get approval for the appointment of a consultant and add it to the overall budget later.

Project length

These are recommended steps to work out a sequential order for the main tasks:

1 LIST ACTIVITIES

As indicated in Chapter 2, pp. 46-63, you can only start to estimate time accurately when you have a detailed list of all the tasks that you must achieve. Imagine a multinational food retailer is planning its first foray into China. A list of tasks could include: 'buying or renting an office in Beijing', 'finding a representative in China' and 'finding a Chinese-speaking coordinator at head office'. Short phrases with active verbs are easier to understand.

2 ESTIMATE TIMES

Next, you need to estimate how much time each activity is likely to take. This is where you have to refer to your list of sources and work out which is going to give you the most accurate description. For instance, for 'finding a Chinese-speaking coordinator at head office', you need to find out basic details such as: how long does it take to put an ad in the paper for a local Chinese speaker, how long do you give candidates to apply, when is the earliest time you can set an interview date, how soon could the chosen candidate be hired? If you have problems coming up with a specific time, include the earliest and latest possible time estimates.

3 CONNECT ACTIVITIES
Once you have made a list of activities with estimates of the time that each activity will take, you can start thinking about how the activities are connected to each other. Activities that need to be completed in a sequence, with each stage being more-or-less completed before the next activity can begin are known as dependent or sequential. Other activities are not dependent on completion of any other tasks. These may be done at any time before or after a particular stage is reached. These are non-dependent or 'parallel' tasks.

4 PRIORITIZE TASKS

For instance, you need to ask yourself whether it's necessary to find a Chinese-speaking coordinator at the head office before making appointments in China itself. Or you can consider whether some members of the team can travel to China to look at property and search for a China representative at the same time as the search at the head office takes place. Does one activity depend on the other? By evaluating these options, you should be closer to prioritizing tasks. You might decide, for instance, that you would save a lot of time and money if a Chinese-speaking person is hired at headquarters to arrange the search in China, even if it means waiting a month, for instance, until that key person is hired.

5 CREATE A NETWORK DIAGRAM

A network diagram or flow chart is a popular method used to help you connect activities and to see how activities depend on each other.

On a blank piece of paper, place your activities in different parts of the paper and circle them. The tasks that can be undertaken simultaneously can be shaded in red, for instance, while the activities that can only begin when other activities have been completed can be shaded in yellow. Show how the tasks are connected to each other with arrows, and next to the arrows write down the duration of each task. The network diagram you create should help you to see a critical path – and to see the sequence of activities that takes the longest time to complete as well as the non-critical tasks that can be delayed by some amount of time. Critical paths are not set in stone and will change as more tasks are inserted or deleted.

In the diagram opposite, which ends with the white circle, Search for offices in Beijing, tasks joined by darker arrows are critical. Those joined by lighter arrows are non-critical.

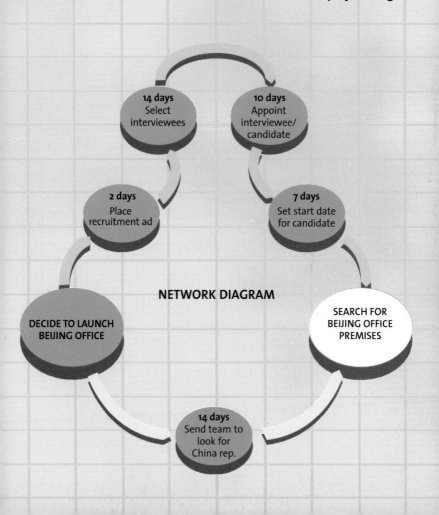

NETWORK DIAGRAM

14 days
Select interviewees

10 days
Appoint interviewee/ candidate

2 days
Place recruitment ad

7 days
Set start date for candidate

DECIDE TO LAUNCH BEIJING OFFICE

SEARCH FOR BEIJING OFFICE PREMISES

14 days
Send team to look for China rep.

estimating time, resources and money

Setting dates

Once you have calculated how the activities in the project are connected, what order they need to follow and the minimum and maximum durations, you are closer to being able to set actual dates.

1 WRITE DOWN CRUX DATES
Although key dates may not have emerged at this stage of the project, there may be some dates that are more or less fixed. For instance, if you are working for a customer that needs certain merchandise in time for the summer sales or for Christmas, then you know that key dates, in June and December respectively, are the last possible dates for delivery. Similarly, if you know a rival is also planning to enter China by a particular date or that a local Chinese company has set dates for its launch, then you have a more or less fixed deadline if the company is going to enter the market competitively.

2 CALCULATE ACTIVITY DATES

Even if you have no fixed key dates, it's useful to impose some sort of deadline so that you can have a hypothetical scenario to work against. Creating a Gantt chart is a useful way to schedule when key tasks will be carried out and to allow you to plan the allocation of resources needed to complete the project. At its most basic level, you create a chart by listing in vertical order on the left-hand side of a sheet all the main activities. Then, horizontally across the page you create a time scale for the project that is based on the crux dates or hypothetical dates. If the time scale is 12 weeks for instance, you can assign smaller periods of weeks (duration time) to each activity.

3 FILL IN THE CHART

The chart will allow you to see clearly which activity will take longest and where in the time sequence it will begin. For instance, hiring a Chinese-speaking coordinator has a time span of four weeks at the beginning of the project whereas the purchasing activity of property in China may take longer, nine weeks for example, because completion of the task is dependent on more factors (and is therefore less controllable) than making a new appointment.

GANTT CHART

PROJECT: LAUNCHING A CHINESE OPERATION/OFFICE										
ACTIVITY/TASK	TIME/WEEKS									
	1	2	3	4	5	6	7	8	9	10
Put recruitment ad in newspaper/website	■									
Set up interview		■								
Make appointment of home-based China representative			■							
Find China-based coordinator					■	■	■	■	■	■
Buy/rent office in Beijing					■	■	■	■	■	■

☐ Bar=duration of task

4 REVIEW TIMING
A Gantt chart will show clearly how some activities overlap each other and this enables you to check whether the same resources can be used for the activities or whether you have to shift the timing of one of the activities. For instance, if finding property in China is pivotal to the project but key team members can't travel to China because they are involved in a domestic part of the project (overlap), then you might be able to find other people to replace them at the head office. You may also find you can postpone non-critical activities till the end of the project to ensure all energies are focused on the core business.

5 GAIN AGREEMENT
Schedules may look perfect in theory, but you must make
sure that all team members are available for those dates and
for the duration (as some may be part-time). If people aren't
available, you may have to recruit new people. You should also
allow some slack time in the schedule for hold-ups, overruns,
quality rejections, failures in delivery, accidents and
emergencies, holidays and meetings.

Project resources

The project's performance relies on your skills in recruiting the best possible team to carry out the necessary activities. You have to play a delicate balancing act where you push for the best human resources to ensure quality and speed without putting too much burden on the budget. Inevitably, compromises are necessary. Before worrying too much about expenses, draw up the ideal scenario for your project team that can then be thinned down according to the budget requisites. The following are tips to help you identify the best people for the roles.

1 LIST SKILLS NEEDED
Write a list of key roles for the project and next to it the name of the position, a position description and a list of skills. In the case of the retailer planning to enter China, the name of the position at the head office is 'supervisor', a position description would be 'supervising a team to open a store in Beijing' and skills will include 'Chinese speaker and previous supervisory experience'. You might decide that work experience outside your home country is a bonus but not essential. Make a distinction between necessary and preferred skills.

2 CHECK TEAM LOGIC

Once you've made your list, place the different roles in logical clusters and groups and analyze the logic of the groups. Do the roles complement each other? Is there a link missing? For instance, is the new Chinese-speaking supervisor going to work alone or with the help of an assistant? Is there a person earmarked to do the assistant work? Or could this be done part time? Will the supervisor be expected to travel and do the research in China or will he or she just be coordinating, which means another person will have to be hired in China? The example shows how one appointment can have an impact on other hiring.

3 LOOK AT THE AVAILABLE WORK POOL

Although you want the best available candidate, you have to know the constraints. For instance, the budget for new appointments might be very low. Will you have to make the best of existing staff and train the chosen candidates for the project role rather than advertize externally? In the case of the retailer, the necessity of a Chinese language skill may mean an external candidate is essential.

4 WORK OUT AVAILABILITY

Even when you do have your best available candidate, the timing may be wrong. Can the project's timing be changed to accommodate the chosen person? This is a rare luxury in the majority of projects.

5 GET AGREEMENTS

Once you've established who can do the work and when, you still need to firm up commitments, both from players and their supervisors in the case of employees who are already in the company and have other responsibilities.

These agreements can be formalized in a commitment matrix that reminds all stakeholders of their responsibilities towards the project. In organizations with formal processes, you may also need to get an investment appraisal (or cost-benefit analysis) signed off.

Project costs

A project budget provides an estimate of the costs of all resources needed to carry out your project. The budget will include the following details:

DIRECT COSTS

These are costs that are directly linked to the project activity and will include:

- Salaries: any extra pay negotiated for you in the specific role of project manager (and not for your usual post in the company) and other company members brought in for the project.

- Equipment: stationery, computers and other materials purchased or loaned for the project.

- Travel: any travel expenses incurred during the project.

- Subcontracts: this includes any external services commissioned for the project.

CALCULATING DIRECT COSTS

If you assume that any extra-pay salaries and subcontracts will be payable by the hour or by the day – the most likely scenario – you should be able to use the schedule plan to calculate roughly how many hours each team member will work on the project.

In the same way, you should already have an idea of how much travel will be necessary and how much it will cost. Don't wait for individuals to set up travel itineraries before you find out the cost.

For jobs paid for the work done rather than for the hours taken, make sure the amount paid reflects the time you have estimated that it will take to carry out.

INDIRECT COSTS

Expenditures that aren't directly linked to the project, but that are related, are indirect costs. They include administrative costs – secretaries, receptionists, general support staff and cleaners who already work in the company but who are also being used for the project. Ongoing overheads such as rental of office space, postage, furniture and general office supplies are also indirect costs because they are shared by the company and the project team.

CALCULATING INDIRECT COSTS

Indirect costs are rather more complicated to track down. You have to check with senior management to determine whether the overall budget will take into account the fact that you are using some of the existing materials and services of the company. Don't assume that you will just be able to have access to and use the main company resources.

CONTINGENCY FUNDS

Senior management and sponsors are likely to downplay the need for emergency funds, but you must factor in any possible mishaps during the project so you are not caught by surprise if things go wrong. Be prepared to map out a response to a worst-case scenario. For instance, if the food retailer does go ahead with the store opening in Beijing but unexpected political developments lead to a six-month delay, how will this affect revenue? Can you estimate losses based on projected sales? Will you have to release staff? Can the company afford to wait for the situation to clear up? In this case, as project manager, you are doing more than simply forecasting the future, you are already setting up potential contingency plans.

Checklist: estimates

1 Goal posts often move in the preliminary stages of planning a project. Have you noted any shift in the parameters and checked that you aren't making calculations based on an out-of-date list of activities? ☐

2 Have you made promises to a client that you can't realistically keep just to make him or her happy? Is your deadline optimistic? ☐

3 Have you done extensive research that will help you to assess how much time the project will take and how much it will cost? ☐

4 Are you using various sources for your research? Could you be relying too much on either your experience or written documents? Should you double-check with another colleague or a consultant? ☐

5 When calculating the estimated time a task can take, have you included the best and worst possible scenarios? ☐

6 Are you aware of the difference between 'dependent' and 'non-dependent' activities and how they affect the preparation of a schedule? ☐

7 Have you been able to pin down some approximate dates for the start and closure of the project? Or at least, to create a feasible set of dates to devise a timeline? ☐

8 Do you have a list of clearly defined roles? ☐

CHECKLIST

9 Have you worked out how team members will work within their smaller groups or specialities? Are there any missing links?

☐

10 Have you confirmed that all project candidates are free to work on the project on the chosen dates?

☐

11 Have you worked out the total direct costs of the project?

☐

12 Have you worked out a formula with senior management about how to calculate indirect costs?

☐

13 Have you got final approval of the budget from senior management/the sponsor, either in the form of a commitment matrix or an investment appraisal? ☐

14 Have you taken into account any of the potential pitfalls you may face during the project? ☐

15 Do you have a contingency plan if your worst-case scenario in fact happens? ☐

16 Do you have extra funds to finance a contingency plan? ☐

17 Are your monitoring systems up and running? ☐

CHECKLIST

4

building a project team

building a project team

Team essentials

A project plan may look highly effective on paper, but its success will depend on the quality of the project team implementing it. Therefore, a thorough understanding of all the project team's responsibilities and skills is crucial.

THE PROJECT MANAGER'S ROLE
The following cover most of the main responsibilities of a project manager:

1 Preparing a master plan

2 Establishing objectives

3 Drawing up a schedule

4 Fixing a budget

5 Communicating the team members' roles to them

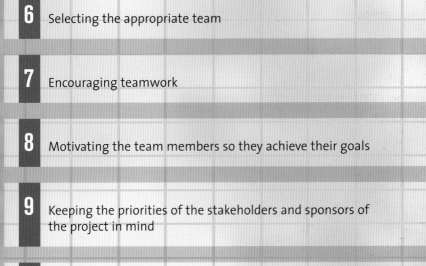

6 Selecting the appropriate team

7 Encouraging teamwork

8 Motivating the team members so they achieve their goals

9 Keeping the priorities of the stakeholders and sponsors of the project in mind

10 Juggling their demands with the challenges facing the team

11 Monitoring progress

12 Ensuring targets are met

ASSESSING YOUR SKILLS AND COMMITMENT

If you are uncertain about your readiness to manage a project, answer the following questions. If the majority of the answers are positive, then you are confident in your role. If they are negative, there are some leadership skills you can develop:

1 Are you prepared to carry the blame if the project fails?

2 Do you have a personal as well as business interest in this project?

3 Do you like motivating people?

4 Do you like seeing your team develop?

5 Can you cope with changes to a structure after it has been approved?

6 Are you good at delegating tasks to others?

building a project team

Different styles of leadership

Most managers fit into one of the following categories of leadership styles and many will have to change their style according to the circumstances and the team members they are dealing with.

1

AUTHORITARIAN
This leadership style involves having a firm rein on staff, making most decisions on your own and discouraging different ways of looking at things. This dictatorial style is most prevalent in times of crisis when there is no time for consensus or when a radical plan that faces stiff opposition is being implemented. Managers can pull this approach off if they have charisma or have unusual persuasive powers. The greatest disadvantage is that team members can get very disgruntled if they are in opposition and are unable to vent their opinions.

2 HANDS-ON

Keeping a close eye on fellow workers does not necessarily mean you are being authoritarian. It may merely indicate that the project tasks are complicated and possibly novel for the company and that you need to be the sort of manager who checks developments regularly and encourages less-confident workers.

3 CONSENSUS-SEEKING
When a project's objectives have been widely approved
from the outset, a manager can afford to spend more time
listening to different views, both of subordinates and
sponsors. Also referred to as 'democratic', 'sympathetic' or
'patient', this approach is particularly effective in building
team confidence and encouraging team members to use
their own initiative. The downside of an opinion-seeking
approach is that sometimes it takes too long to make a
decision, with negative effects on the project.

4 ANALYTICAL

Some managers prefer to spend more time analysing the plan, fine-tuning decisions and gathering facts than goading team workers. This may indicate they are familiar with their team workers and have confidence in their own initiatives. Or they may have been hired specifically for their attention to detail. These leaders will have to be good at delegating.

building a project team

Functional roles

The following list includes all the people who are likely to take part in the project in one way or another and whose help or advice you will turn to at some stage – albeit small – of the project. It is not limited to those team members who you have specifically hired for the project:

PROJECT CHAMPION

Ideally, by the time you are close to completing the project plan, you will already have identified the person who strongly supports your project. This person will probably be a senior director in your company or an influential outsider who has a vested interest in the success of your project. The project champion may not necessarily be involved in the nitty gritty details of the day-to-day operation but can always be relied upon for advice and support, perhaps even as a powerful leverage during tough times.

SENIOR DIRECTOR

Although, as project manager, you may hold a senior position in the company, it is probable that another senior, if not more senior, official will have the final say on major issues like budget approvals and strategic decisions.

IDEA ORIGINATOR

The person who came up with the idea in the first place could be the project champion, the senior director or be an external source.

In any case, it is important to have the person onboard if only to refer to during the project for advice and secondary support.

PROJECT SUPERVISOR

Although you are the main leader of the project, you will undoubtedly need the support of at least one project supervisor to oversee the day-to-day operations that you may not necessarily have time for. Don't be afraid to delegate. In fact, it's essential that you divide activities between you. Divide tasks up evenly into areas such as salaries, holidays, time-keeping, measuring activities, arranging meetings, and stick to the agreed tasks.

TEAM MEMBERS

Depending on the project, you will recruit different directors according to their expertise. These could already be working for the company or be hired as freelancers. Although you want to make sure that all members are in agreement with the general direction of the project, you don't necessarily want all 'yes' people. It's useful to include one or two more independent-minded members who question decisions and are able to offer an alternative way of thinking to the majority.

COMPANY STAFF

Existing company departments, including human resources, accountancy, legal and finance are considered company staff. They will have to be onboard for the day-to-day running of the project, especially making and taking in payments, without being involved in the strategic side of the plan. You will require diplomacy and tact when seeking their logistical support while fending off any interference they may want to make in the day-to-day running of the operation.

CLIENTS

If the company provides specific products or services, their end users will be invaluable contributors to the team to test ideas and to provide opinions on results. The ultimate success of the company's products will depend largely on their acceptance and satisfaction ratings so it's crucial to involve them at every possible stage of the project and to elicit, listen to and act upon their feedback, both positive and negative.

ANALYSTS

External advisers or opinion formers can offer further input to the project. They are especially useful when nobody in the team has had sufficient experience with the particular problem you are dealing with or, on the opposite extreme, a key project sponsor has managed similar problems so many times before that he or she may be lacking a fresh perspective or approach. It is important always to be aware of the background and potential bias of any analysts or consultants you use.

Team roles

Regardless of their functional roles in the project, key team members also tend to play a secondary role in the project by playing team roles that should complement each other and further the project's goals. In making appointments, a project manager may subconsciously look at the different roles team members can play:

NIT-PICKER/CRITIC

Excessive criticism can demotivate staff members, but it can also be very useful to have a 'nit-picker' in the team who has unrealistically high standards. The project manager doesn't have to agree with many of the observations, but it is useful to compare ongoing results with the perfect vision that is often provided by an obsessively critical team member.

TEAM BUILDER

An enthusiastic team member who thrives on collective tasks and bringing people together can inject much-needed team spirit into a project, in particular on those occasions when the project manager is not around to provide it.

CREATIVE

Imaginative people can sometimes be unrealistic and they can upset a schedule with their improvised way of working, but it is invaluable to have an ideas person on the team who thinks outside the box.

ACTIVATOR

Some people are less interested in the ideas and keener to push things forward. Usually brimming with energy and goal-oriented, these people, also known as implementers, will tend to hurry the critics and creatives and make sure that the team is aware of pending deadlines.

CARER

An array of personalities working to a tight schedule are liable to fight, and this can slow a project down. To have a sympathetic person who listens to grievances without getting personally involved can help to diffuse many situations and act as a safety valve for the more volatile members.

Appointing the team

Once you have identified the key people you want to be involved in your team, you need to make sure you can obtain their participation. These are some guidelines to secure their involvement:

1 WRITE A LIST
To make sure you have covered all the tasks, prepare a list of different functions and roles, with brief descriptions of each task.

■ Assign an activity name and number that you can refer to once the project is underway and that also explains the function of the role.

■ Include start and end dates and the number of hours the task is expected to take.

■ On the opposite side of the page, for each job, assign potential candidates with contact details.

■ Make sure you have a backup for each candidate, in case your first choice is not available.

2 CONTACT THE CANDIDATE
As soon as the project plans are approved:

■ Contact your preferred candidates to inform them that you've been given the green light and are ready to sign a work agreement or contract.

■ Go through the list and confirm future participation. Many projects don't get underway until several months after you originally contacted the candidates.

■ Chase your second choice immediately if first-choice candidates are no longer available for work.

3 CONFIRM THE PROJECT ROLE
When you have lined up the candidates:

■ Confirm with them that they understand the exact nature of the work you expect from them.

■ To avoid confusion, put any descriptions of the task and deadlines on paper and get a signed agreement.

4 ARRANGE A TEAM MEETING
Although some team members will come onboard at different times during the project, sometimes several weeks after the start-up, it's useful to have a preliminary meeting to gather all team members together.

5 COMMUNICATE OBJECTIVES AND ROLES

- Go through the objectives of the project, the nature of the activities and look into how they will overlap. This may be the only time the entire team will meet until the project wrap-up.

- Ask members to introduce themselves and to explain their roles. By forcing them to speak in public about their participation, you can make sure that they have fully understood their role. It also gives other members a better idea of whom they are going to work with.

6 COMMUNICATE THE SCHEDULE

- By the end of the meeting circulate a project schedule that alerts all members as to the proposed milestones and deadlines they have to meet.

Fostering teamwork – stages

A team spirit is not created automatically; it has to be nurtured. It may help you to encourage teamwork if you are aware of some of the typical stages most teams go through in the life of a project.

1 FORMING

At the outset, some team members won't be fully committed to the project, and others will feel insecure about their roles. In smaller groups than in the initial meeting, discussed on the previous page, give people another opportunity to introduce themselves formally and to explain their functions, discuss their expectations and reveal something of their background and areas of expertise.

2 STORMING

In spite of best intentions, conflict and clashes are inevitable after the initial breaking-in period, if only because different members are jockeying for position and testing each other's limits. As project manager, it is your responsibility to steer as many of these discussions as possible into an open forum to help keep them from getting too personal and to help negotiate a solution. Often these 'storming' clashes arise out of individual members' fears and insecurities about how effectively they are carrying out their assigned tasks.

3 NORMING
Once concerns have been aired, a period of stabilization should follow, where operating guidelines, such as the setting of deadlines or the setting up of meetings, are established.

4 PERFORMING
Ideally, the team should be cooperating and working towards a shared objective as soon as possible. As this stage can't be guaranteed, the project manager must motivate players into working together. Financial incentives are tricky motivators because the project manager doesn't necessarily have any authority over payments. However, project managers do have control over other incentives such as recognizing good work, granting more responsibilities, promising more work in the future and encouraging people to develop their skills.

5 BORING
This stage occurs in particularly long projects and emerges
when people in the team think the project is stalling or
believe they have outlasted their role. When the end still
seems out of sight, the project manager must remind the
team of deadlines and pending targets.

6 MOURNING
During a long project, some key members finish their tasks
before others, which can be destabilizing when a particular
group has bonded well. The project manager has to watch out
for any period of grieving, perhaps by introducing additional
responsibilities or challenges to coincide with the departure of
a popular team member.

How to delegate effectively

Delegating work to team members is one of the greatest challenges for project managers because many people think that it is giving control and power away. Try to look at this process in a more positive light. When you are overseeing a project, you are inevitably going to have to focus more on some tasks than others, and by delegating work, you can free yourself up. Also, by handing out work to a trusted colleague, you are helping to foster teamwork and to build up an individual's confidence and expertise. The following steps can help to minimize the risks many managers fear when delegating work.

1 CHOOSE SENSIBLY

Seek out the person in the team with the best track record rather than potential because your priority is to have a safe pair of hands on the task. Don't go for the big ideas person; when you want something done, it is safer to go for the person who follows procedures. This part of the project (once most of the plan has been conceived) is not the time to encourage new ideas that are going to alter the original plan.

It's useful to keep a detailed list of employees, their strengths and weaknesses and how long they have been in the company. When a new assignment or project comes up, you can make a quick decision based on recent evidence and availability. Employees are more likely to be impressed with your hands-on knowledge of their work.

2 COMMUNICATE CLEARLY

It is important to have a meeting with the chosen person as to the exact nature and goals of the task and to follow this up in writing.

Clear communication will avoid facing typical pleas of ignorance like: 'I was never told that was the deadline. Did you send it to the right e-mail address?'

3 SET REALISTIC TARGETS

If you were originally expecting to do the task yourself, you may have to add some more time to allow the newly assigned person to come to grips with the new role.

4 MONITOR PROGRESS
As with the project plan, milestones should be clearly indicated so that the appointed person has a way of checking actual progress with stated goals.

5 GET FEEDBACK
Seek updates on how the person you've appointed is performing. Encourage the person to report back on a regular basis, and ask trusted colleagues who are directly affected to give you a quick impression. However, there is no substitute for spending some time checking results and intervening if problems build up.

6 ENCOURAGE ACCOUNTABILITY
Even as a project manager, you may not necessarily have direct authority over the people to whom you have delegated some work. Neither can you expect them to share the responsibility with you if, in the worst-case scenario, something goes wrong. Try to confirm the appointment with each person's direct supervisor (if they have been asked to work on the project on a part-time basis). That way you have more leverage to negotiate more commitment and time from your team members in the inevitable periods when their project tasks clash with another assignment.

How to motivate the team

Encouraging team members is one of the project manager's key responsibilities. These are some tips to follow:

1 QUESTION MOTIVATION
Think of the different reasons why your employees are doing their jobs. The most enthusiastic simply relish a challenge, others are merely interested in the salary and security, others are keen on a bonus and some want the status of the job. You can't expect all team members to be as committed to the project as you are. Be aware of what makes each individual tick, and act accordingly. In general, demand high standards of them, and you are more likely to encourage hard work.

2 RECOGNIZE GOOD WORK

Too many managers are willing to speak out when work is going badly, but they will say nothing when targets are made. People don't like to hear only negative criticism, and once they are branded as ineffective, they can lose self-confidence and goodwill. Credit them for a task well done. Be specific about your compliment – it will show you have an eye for detail and that you have really taken notice. It may also offset any future negative criticism of their work.

3 STEER THEM THROUGH THE FEAR OF CHANGE

Most projects strive for changing established routines. Even if the original routines were unpopular, shifting the landscape can be unsettling for employees. Project managers who are aware of the three common phases during a period of change will be able to provide the best support to their team.

Initially, the most common response to the introduction of new measures is resistance. People fear that their position within the department or company will be in jeopardy and that their workload will increase. It helps if you point out the cons of the old system and the pros of the new system – for instance, greater efficiency and a smaller workload.

4 ENCOURAGE POSITIVE CHANGE
Try to identify the employees who are embracing the change and see if they can be recruited to promote the new system in a persuasive way. Think of examples where competitors have made similar changes with successful results. There must also be negative examples of companies that resisted change and may have been forced to shut down.

5 SET UP APPRAISALS
During a project when all members are involved in new tasks, it is useful to have appraisals more regularly, even on a weekly basis. Focus on planned objectives, and seek evidence for how employees met their targets. Try not to linger on subjective subjects like initiative, judgement or attitude. These are difficult to quantify and can become highly personal. Stick to hard facts.

Checklist: teambuilding

1 Can you list the three main responsibilities given to the project manager? ☐

2 Are you aware of the different leadership styles you can adopt, and are you able to mix styles according to the situation? ☐

3 In building up your team, do you have enough support, from senior management or other people with power, for your decisions? ☐

4 When building a team, have you made sure that, apart from filling the functional and technical roles, you have also tried to mix different personalities who will complement each other in your team? ☐

5 Have you written accurate and clear descriptions of each team member's role? ☐

6 Have you set up adequate check points or methods of measuring performance? ☐

7 Are all team members aware, in writing, of the project schedule and co-workers' responsibilities? ☐

8 Have you paid enough attention to the first stages of fostering teamwork? Are you sure all players are comfortable in their new roles? ☐

9 Are you aware of the different options available to motivate team members? ☐

CHECKLIST

5

launching the project

Halfway point

There is no exact halfway point in a project. Every project is unique and varies in scope and length, and managers will choose their own halfway point where they can sit back and reflect on the progress so far. However, there is a natural pause in most projects that takes place between the period of planning and the moment of final approval, which precedes putting the project into action. This pre-launch period is normally an ideal time to look back at the progress made so far and to assess pending assignments.

1

WHAT ARE THE MAIN CONSTRAINTS OF THE PROJECT?
If you decide the objectives are as pressing now as they were at the start of the project, have you identified all the potential obstacles to the project? Establish if:

- The costs of establishing links with sportswear producers are prohibitive.
- The focus on a new line of clothing will harm relations with other existing clothing clients and suppliers.
- There are too many changes to make to your existing transport infrastructure.

2 WHAT IS THE REASON FOR YOUR PROJECT?
You may feel it is unnecessary at this stage to return to the definition. You may fear that the definition is no longer valid and be unwilling to confront this. But if the goal posts have genuinely moved a long way – for instance, if a competitor has decided to take the same action as you – this is the time to realize it and decide either to abandon the project or to spend more time refining it. Otherwise, it can act as a reminder for you and the team of your project's purpose. Try to answer the following questions:

- What was the problem that led the company to decide a project was necessary? In the case of the supplier of men's apparel, it was the dwindling demand for men's traditional formal casual wear.
- Who suggested instigating change? For instance, was the supplier's major client – a well-known department store – the originator of the idea to make a foray into sports leisure wear? If so, are they still convinced this is a growth market?
- Who will be the main beneficiaries of the project? In this case, is it the department store? The clothing supplier?
- What would happen if the project were shelved? Would it adversely affect the bottom line? Would it mean a significant loss of revenue?

3

WHO HAVE YOU INVOLVED IN THE PROJECT?
Make sure you know who's on board, who will support you
during tough times, and monitor their mood. Confirm that:

- You can name all the key players who will play a significant
  role in the project, such as the champion of the project. In
  the case of the men's clothing supplier, this is the
  department store.
- You also have the backing of senior management so you
  won't be facing any negative consequences of the project
  on your own.
- These key players are still as enthusiastic about the project
  as they were at the outset.

4 WHAT ARE THE DESIRED OUTCOMES OF THE PROJECT?
In the case of the clothing supplier, the results of the project will mean that the company has diversified into the growing sports apparel market, to complement its main business – the supply of men's traditional casual wear. The company's new line is expected to spearhead growth and to compensate for smaller demand for traditional casual wear. The move could also potentially lead to a new contract with several small shops.

5 HAVE YOU IDENTIFIED ALL THE RESOURCES YOU WILL NEED?
Do you have:

- A list of the number of employees who will participate in the project?
- Their starting and finishing dates (if recruited externally)?
- The financing (either from inside the company or from a client) for the extra staff you will need for an agreed period of time?
- The financing to rent or buy new equipment?
- A clear idea that you won't have to turn to any new resources at the last minute?

6 DO YOU HAVE A LIST OF ALL THE ACTIVITIES THAT NEED TO TAKE PLACE?
You should have a nearly complete list of the tasks that need
to be done and a list of staff who are going to carry them out.
The details on the list should include a description of the
projected target and deadlines for tasks to be completed.

7 WHAT ABOUT THE MONITORING AND CLOSE-DOWN REPORT?
Have you:

■ Arranged a comprehensive and efficient way of monitoring
all the activities once the project has been launched? (See
Chapter 6, pp. 152-209 for more details.)
■ Already thought about certain aspects of the close-down
report? (See Chapter 7, pp. 210-235 for more details.)

Analysis complete?

You should have answered the questions in the halfway point analysis positively and vowed to resolve any negatives shortly. It may seem you are now ready for the final launch, but there are still a few isolated tasks, which are not part of the project tasks, that you need to do to smooth out the implementation stage. These tasks are examined in this chapter:

1 Handling uncertainties

2 Managing information

3 Communicating effectively

4 Preparing a project report

HANDLING UNCERTAINTIES

It's easy at this stage to brush off any imponderables about the potential risk of your project, but it is much safer to identify them and to be prepared to combat them if they do emerge. These are some steps to follow to convince yourself and your stakeholders that you are ready to handle uncertainties:

1 ASK 'WHAT IF?' QUESTIONS
Be prepared to map out a response to a worst-case scenario. For instance, if a competitor launches a similar project at the same time, what kind of impact will this have on the objectives? Or what will happen if the project is delayed by six months? How will customers respond? Are there alternative paths you could follow?

2 WORK OUT ODDS
What are the odds of each outcome being played out? If you find this difficult, use your judgement, do some research or turn to experts. Try to be specific, for example, by using a percentage or a decimal; do not use a vague phrase like 'quite likely'.

3 ASSESS SUCCESS
You can also try using probability theory to lower the element of error. You do this by working out the likelihood of an event happening on a scale of 0 (impossible) to 1 (guaranteed) with a 50/50 chance of success scoring at 0.5. You can then multiply the set of possible investments by these probabilities to gauge which ones give you the better figures.

4 IDENTIFY KEY UNCERTAINTIES
Not all uncertainties will have a major impact on the future, so it's a good idea to chose three to five risky scenarios and describe the ways they could affect the project.

5 PRIORITIZE
Try to single out the most important uncertainty. Or take each uncertainty at a time and describe the way it could impinge on the decision.

6 SPECIFY IMPACT
Refine a list of possible outcomes and describe them. Make sure that the chosen outcomes clearly differ from each other, include all possible scenarios and are clearly defined.

7 SIMULATE THE FUTURE
You can try to enact the future using computer programs that work out complex equations and run through a range of positive and negative possible scenarios. Computer graphics will help to illustrate the points to other staff members.

8 HIRE CONSULTANTS
You can turn to experts with both the know-how and experience when in-house resources are unable to carry out complicated calculations.

9 CONTINGENCY PLANS

Imagine the worst-case scenario, and think of at least two ways to respond. For instance, if a competitor enters China before your company, would you:

■ Abandon the project altogether?
■ Decide to launch in a new city that has no competition?
■ Stick to the original plan but allocate extra resources for marketing?

MANAGING INFORMATION

After the project is formally launched and time pressures intensify, it will become more challenging to relay information to all team members. Also, the information already available will be changing far more quickly as activities are completed, new challenges emerge and outcomes are achieved. These are some suggestions to upgrade information as efficiently as possible and to ensure dissemination is smooth.

1

SET UP A PHYSICAL INFORMATION CENTRE

The size and scope of an information centre will depend on the size and scope of the project. For a medium- to large-sized company, it is useful to have at least a room allocated as an information centre or a mini-reference library quite separate from any existing company library. At the very least, a computer that is easy to access for all office members can act as an information centre.

2 SEPARATE THE DATA

Dividing data into files and subfiles is a tidy and efficient way of grouping information. Start with two basic sections, one related to the project's schedule and vision statement and the second to supporting material. Further divisions could include completed work, activities in progress and pending tasks.

3 APPOINT A KNOWLEDGE COORDINATOR

In an ideal scenario, team members will make sure they file data themselves as they go along, but the reality is that the best intentions begin well and then flounder under pressures of time, laziness and habit.

If the budget permits it, you should make one person responsible for the project data, both to harangue members to keep updating information and to chase people with deadlines on reports.

Even when resources are scant, it pays in the long run to appoint a coordinator on a part-time basis. Make sure that the person hired is aware of his or her responsibilities and that the remuneration is sufficient to ensure that the work is carried out.

COMMUNICATING EFFECTIVELY

A project will flow more easily and swiftly if communication channels are efficient. These are some guidelines for effective communication.

1

ASK QUESTIONS

It is mainly up to you as the project manager to encourage open communication. There is no substitute for asking plenty of questions and making yourself as available as possible both to team members and to sponsors and senior directors.

2

MAKE ANNOUNCEMENTS

Think of your role as a daily broadcaster of news. Aim to make frequent announcements. People like to be kept informed of developments and, consequently, will spend more valuable time seeking it out. Be brief, to the point and light. The last thing members need is an overload of information and irrelevant data.

3 LISTEN

How do you show people that you are really listening?

- Use body language to show you are paying attention. For instance, lean your body slightly forwards, nod your head at regular intervals and keep eye contact.

- Don't interrupt unless you are checking to verify a certain point or word you don't understand.

- Repeat what the person is saying in your own words to make sure you've got it right. For instance, say: 'Just to make sure I've understood. You're saying that...' or 'Can you clarify that last point?'

- Avoid answering any phone calls during a meeting, unless it's an emergency. Taking notes helps people feel you are taking them seriously. It also provides a useful reference if the problem can't be resolved immediately.

4 PREPARE WEEKLY REPORTS

Weekly reports can serve as useful updates (see Chapter 6, pp. 158-161). They differ from a start-up report, which is specifically prepared before the launch period and is discussed on the next page.

PREPARING A PROJECT REPORT

A start-up report provides the project manager with an opportunity to summarize the project's objectives, constraints and targets as well as to create a document that serves as a kick-off to the next phase: the launch.

A report is also the final confirmation that all participants have agreed on the procedures to be followed; therefore, it's a useful document to get signed by all key stakeholders.

The ideal platform to launch the start-up report is a meeting attended by all team members. The agenda of the launch meeting can be taken from the report.

The start-up report should include the following details:

1 LIST THE STAKEHOLDERS
As the project manager, you are probably one of the few members of the project team who has met all participants, including the sponsors and/or customers who are involved at arm's length. A list of all so-called stakeholders is a useful reference tool.

2 LAUNCH THE PROJECT
Invite all stakeholders to the launch meeting, and ask them to introduce themselves briefly as you go down the list. This helps to break the ice and also lets team members know that there is outside interest and support for the project.

3 PROJECT A VISION
As project manager, you need to spell out why the company is keen to pursue this project and what the main objectives and benefits of the project will be for the company. Ask a couple of the key stakeholders to contribute their vision of the project to support your introductory statement and perhaps to provide variety and credibility to the project.

4 ESTABLISH TARGETS
List the main outcomes that the project is striving for – this will instill a sense of urgency. Team members should also be motivated when they hear that the company has set up a system of milestones and checks to measure the ongoing achievements of the project.

5 RECOGNIZE UNCERTAINTIES
To inject a dose of reality into the proceedings, you should
include some of the uncertainties in the project. However, as
the launch of a project should start as positively as possible,
try to minimize the risk factors and highlight the ways the
company is planning to overcome any challenges.

6

monitoring the project

Effective monitoring

It's easy to underestimate the amount of work and planning needed to make sure that a project is on track. A common belief is that if the project manager spends months preparing copious plans and has alerted everyone to their roles, then the bulk of the project management process has ended.

What puts many managers off is that while planning a project involves creativity and thinking, the act of monitoring seems more routine – a case of simply ticking the boxes. This is a common misconception.

Keeping track of different activities, solving inevitable hiccups along the way and resolving new conflicts that will emerge will continue to demand ingenuity and imagination.

The most ingenious plans are ineffective if they are not implemented properly by all concerned. There are many advantages in having a comprehensive monitoring system. They include:

1 MEASURES PROGRESS
Unless the system allows the project manager to compare actual achievements with desired results as described in a project plan, no one can know whether the different stages of the plan are working until it is possibly too late.

2 BOOSTS TEAM MORALE
When a team has to jump over several hurdles to achieve a result that seems elusive, it helps overall morale to have an updated report of how the project is developing.

3 ENCOURAGES FLEXIBILITY
Constant and thorough checking of the process allows last-minute changes to be made because of unforeseen external circumstances. Specific milestones can give the project manager sufficient time for flexibility.

4 ASSURES SPONSORS
A progress report goes a long way to allay any fears – real or imagined – of busy sponsors or senior managers.

5 SAFEGUARDS DECISIONS
Inevitably, the project manager must react to any changes in the project created either internally or by competitors. By keeping all key players informed of developments, project managers can cover themselves for any decisions they had to make on the spur of the moment, in case their actions are later questioned.

6 PREVENTS COLLAPSE
In the worst-case scenarios, projects can unravel early on because some obstacles and risks were left unaddressed. Effective monitoring can act as an alert.

Progress reports

One of the most common and convenient ways for project managers to keep tabs on the project – as well as to communicate developments to sponsors, senior managers and team members – is to produce a written project report. The following tips will help you to make sure that your reports contain the necessary information for you to both recognize accomplishments and spot any potential roadblocks:

1 PROVIDE EASY FEEDBACK FORMS

Essential to your report is feedback from the team. The easiest way to get a response is to create a form that is easy for busy employees to fill in. The one-page form should first include straightforward details such as name, department, dates and task names. There could be a space to show what work has been done in the period (for instance, a 'highlights of the week' section), columns with headers such as 'pending obstacles', 'impact', 'suggested action' and 'activities planned for next week', under which team members can easily scribble in any descriptions or recommendations.

2 MAKE REPORTS REGULAR

Reports should appear on a regular basis (preferably weekly) to provide consistency and to encourage contributors not to forget to fill in feedback forms. Midweek is an ideal time to receive a report because it allows participants to discuss any issues in the second half of the week. A weekend report is more likely to be ignored, while at the start of the week, people tend to be busier with 'to-do' lists.

3 MAKE REPORTS BRIEF

Some reports are likely to be longer than others, depending on whether they are targeted to stakeholders, or sponsors, who are both less directly involved with the project (and hence need more information) or to team members, who will have less catching up to do. If you are writing several reports, it's best to write the most detailed one first, which you can then shorten for an internal audience.

4 START WITH HIGHLIGHTS

The report should open with two or three of the most important achievements (or obstacles) of the week, to alert the reader to the most significant points (in the event that they don't read the report through to the end).

5 INCLUDE BASIC DETAILS
A systematic entry of all the basic details makes the report easier to follow. Basics include a list of activities performed, the targets reached or missed, the deadlines met or missed and the state of the budget.

6 MAKE COMPARISONS
Making a list of stated objectives and comparing them to the project's real achievements is a clear and quick way of evaluating how realistic the ambitions of the project are.

7 UNDERLINE PROBLEMS
A report shouldn't include a problem section every week, but if it does, it is clearer to separate these from the basics, because they are not regular features.

Review meetings

A project report, however thorough, is not a sufficient monitoring tool on its own. You need to complement written accounts of developments with face-to-face encounters called review meetings, where participants can air their views openly and where the meeting leader – probably the project manager – can foster teamwork. Other review meetings include smaller gatherings of team members in clusters, perhaps according to specialities or particular needs, and more formal reviews with external participants such as sponsors or clients. The following tips can help you to make the most of these meetings.

1 BOOK A REGULAR MEETING SLOT

Like a project report, it's sensible to hold a team meeting once a week, maybe a day after the release of the report, which can be used as a useful reference tool for discussion.

By fixing a regular time, people can include that period into their weekly schedules and so have no excuse not to participate. Make sure a big enough room is booked for these meetings.

2 BE SPECIFIC

During busy schedules – invariably the norm for a project –
you should try to stick rigidly to concerns about the progress
of the project in terms of achievements, obstacles and targets.
Don't let the meeting become a forum for general discussion.

3 STRUCTURE THE MEETING

A logical next step to remaining focused is to organize the
meeting around, for instance, the project report, which means
you can systematically work down the list of main concerns
even if there are no pending issues with one or more of the
areas on the list.

4 APPOINT A MEETING LEADER

As project manager, you want time to listen carefully to all the comments, and you want to remain as neutral as possible. It's a good idea to appoint another team member to take the minutes and to act as a chairperson (or better, assign team members to this task on a rotational basis).

The chairperson should insist on punctuality and be tough on latecomers. He or she should make sure that all participants – particularly the shyer ones – contribute. In this case, it's easier to ask specific questions rather than to encourage people to air general opinions.

The chairperson should not be afraid of interrupting if a speaker holds the stage for too long or is rambling away from the subject. It's also useful for the chairperson to intervene at opportune moments with a summary of main points.

5 ALLOW QUESTION TIME
Although you are trying to be specific and stick to the agenda, there are always some questions at the end that might raise more general points about the project, so allow adequate time at the end for a few questions.

6 BE AVAILABLE
Some team members might want to raise individual points with you that they don't have time for during the week, so let the team know you are available for more personal questions for a short while after the meeting.

7 WRITE MEETING SUMMARY
With the notes of the chairperson, write a concise review of the meeting, highlighting, as in the report, the most important issues. Distribute the summary on notice boards, as a memo or via e-mail, no later than a day after the meeting.

E-mail communication

TIPS FOR EFFECTIVE USE OF E-MAIL

E-mail has become an integral part of day-to-day communications for a company, both among workers, often in the same physical office, and between the office and clients and suppliers. Here are some tips for the most effective use of the medium:

1 IS E-MAIL BEST?
Before you even start typing, think whether your request or message is best delivered by e-mail or would it be better to handle your concern with a personal meeting or with a phone call? As a first point of contact, e-mail is increasingly used over other approaches but it is still worth weighing up all your options.

2 KEEP E-MAILS SHORT
The more often people are using e-mail, the more clogged up e-mail addresses are and the less time people can spend pouring over e-mail messages. Keep any communication brief, concise and to the point.

3 READ THROUGH

It's tempting to rifle off a message and to send it immediately, but it is worth spending a few minutes checking outgoing messages, not just for spelling and grammar but also for tone.

4 DON'T SHOUT

Unless you are making a point, don't use capital letters in an e-mail. Many receivers of e-mails see messages written in capitals as aggressive because it looks like the writer is shouting at them.

5 KEEP COPIES

To avoid any misunderstandings and to ensure that you have a record of important communications, always keep a copy of e-mails as you would of significant correspondence.

Monitoring the schedule

The timing of a project almost always presents a challenge. The problem usually stems from the conflicting needs of the end user (client, sponsor or senior manager), who invariably will push for as tight a deadline as possible, and the supplier (the project team), who will insist on more time to create the best possible product.

COMMON CAUSES FOR DELAYS

1 You overestimate the experience of the staff, and as a result you need to spend time (which wasn't allocated in the original plan) on extra training.

2 The level of motivation in the team is not uniform, with the less-enthusiastic team members slowing the process down.

3 Team members fail to record their schedule performance accurately, so you can't identify an operation's slowness early on in the project, when you can potentially do something to speed things up.

4 Personality clashes among members who have never worked together delay the settling-in period.

5 Some activities necessary to the process were left out of the initial project.

6 Some team members are committed to regular work and can spend less time a week on the project than they envisaged.

7 People are being inefficient when they are putting in the allocated time for a task. You didn't factor in the time people spend on peripheral activities that are not directly connected to the task.

MEASURES TO MINIMIZE DELAYS

1 Encourage the use of time sheets. Make sure all members fill them in and return them on a weekly basis. Let team members know that the purpose of the time sheets is to help them gauge how close they are to reaching their targets and to rearrange their schedule if they are having problems. Time sheets are there to assist, not punish people.

Rather than focus solely on the hours worked, ask team members to write down how long each task is taking. It may be useful for future planning to note that a certain activity took longer than usual and to find ways of speeding these tasks up.

2 Arrange weekly face-to-face meetings. If, as project manager, you don't have time, assign a project director to meet with staff so that you get an accurate picture of how long certain tasks are taking.

3 Encourage staff members to suggest ways that could improve their output. Maybe a team is spending an inordinate amount of time photocopying when they could be analyzing some complicated data, which is their real area of expertise.

4 Look at what is really cost-effective. For example, it might be more cost-effective in the long run to hire a temporary worker to cover the clerical work to free team members to focus on their specialities.

5 Don't just look at the time taken to complete an assignment. Judge the work for its quality, not simply the time it took to complete. This is a tricky but necessary balancing act.

Monitoring costs

Like timing, the amount spent on a project is a source of contention between the project manager, who wants to maximize the range of services, personnel and products to ensure a high-quality delivery of the end product, and the end users, who always believe there is a less expensive way of achieving a goal.

COMMON CAUSES FOR OVERSPENDING

1 The amount spent on a range of products hired or bought specifically for the project was under-researched. For instance, the costs for new mobile phone handsets were unnecessarily high because individuals ended up spending little time on the phone. When communication between geographically separate departments was necessary, one mobile phone could have been shared by three people working closely together. Alternatively, installing an extra landline would have proved less expensive.

2 Invoices for services and products were not paid in time because they got lost in paperwork and ended up incurring late-payment charges and interest.

3 Time delays towards the end of the project meant asking certain team members to work extra time for additional pay.

4 The work schedule of certain team members hired exclusively for the project was underestimated; as a result, they were paid high daily freelance rates.

MEASURES TO MINIMIZE COSTS

1 During the planning process, try to get as many bids as possible from potential providers of services and products. Having many to choose from will help you to make an informed decision on price as well as quality.

2 Once you have the bids, don't be afraid to negotiate a price. Know the maximum price that is acceptable to you, and work towards achieving that price. Remember that everything is negotiable – even if you struggle to get the price you want, you may be able to negotiate other terms or conditions that can have favourable financial implications later.

3 When staff have to work overtime or double-time, get to the bottom of why they haven't been able to complete tasks during normal working hours.

4 If staff have too much work to complete during normal working hours, check the time urgency of some of the activities and decide whether work can be postponed to normal working hours (where rate of pay per hour is less).

5 Approaching the close-down process (in Chapter 7, pp. 210-235), some members of staff may have completed their tasks but are still kept on the payroll in case of emergencies or to support other staff who are still finishing tasks. Inquire whether it is cheaper to lay people off early and re-hire them in an emergency or to keep them for the extra time.

6 Once such items as computers, phones and catering services are no longer needed, pay these invoices immediately and make sure the accounts are officially closed. Some shops or companies continue to charge for their products until a member of the company gets a formal petition or notice to close the account.

7 Don't forget the long-term costs of some decisions. You might think you can save money in the short-term by laying people off earlier than expected or by using less-expensive equipment, but think of the money that the company will lose if the quality of the final result is not as high as if more resources had been used. You may have to recall staff or equipment to fix any problems, which will incur extra cost. You may also disappoint a client, which incurs one of the highest costs of all – lost business.

Handling change

A project plan that escapes change is very unusual. For the majority of projects, last-minute tweaks are the norm, whether they are provoked by customers' new requirements, a sponsor's change of mind or the failure of a task for technical reasons. Not only do you, as project manager, have to be alert to change, you have to know how to respond with speed and how to communicate any new developments to the rest of the team. Sometimes, it's the project manager's responsibility to instigate the change. The following tips are aimed at helping you to tackle change as effectively as possible.

1 ASSESS IMPACT
Particularly when the call for changes comes from external sources, such as clients and senior management, you, as the project manager, must evaluate very carefully why you are being asked to implement changes. Together with your team, you should be aware of how timing, the budget and potential targets will be affected by the changes. The same care and attention should be paid to analyzing the impact on the planning stage.

2 GAIN APPROVAL

If, as project manager, you are convinced that the change is indeed necessary and will raise the chances of reaching the project's objective, you need to get the support of your team. Then, to ensure that the changes are permanent, you should get formal approval from senior management and confirmation from the person or division who originally pushed for the change.

3 RESIST CHANGE?
When you and your team are certain that the suggested changes won't improve the project, and that, in fact, they will prove detrimental, it is your duty to resist changes. Make sure that you have thought of alternatives as well as the consequences of not adopting the changes.

4 INSTALL CHANGE
Assuming you embrace the changes, then you will be keen to make sure the necessary alterations are made to the project plan, immediately and in writing. This will mean the addition of any new activity, possible changes to the schedule or budget and a shift in targets.

5 EXPLAIN CHANGE

Don't assume that the rest of the team, as well as supplier and clients working with the project from a distance, will readily accept the changes. You will need to explain the reasons for the changes and underline the benefits of the new measures. Include in any explanations how the changes will affect, if at all, the functions of each division. Be open to any questions, and take time to hear people's concerns.

6 COMMUNICATE CHANGE

Finally, it is a good idea to write a brief report explaining the process of change, reiterating the advantages of the new system and underlining any changes to the operation.

Combating scope creep

'Scope creep' is the term used to describe the process of introducing new parameters and approaches to a completed project plan. The most common example is when a customer or end user, such as a sponsor, asks a question like 'Wouldn't it be better if we did xxxxx?' or 'Would it mess things up too much if we decided to change...'

EFFECTS OF SCOPE CREEP

1 If you accept a new suggestion, however reasonable, you risk derailing the existing project plan that you have worked so hard to create. The suggestion may appear innocuous, but it's surprising how a few apparently minor changes can force major changes in timing and budget.

2 Accepting a suggestion can encourage a client to make further suggestions, and, before you know it, the entire objective of the project has moved on dramatically but you are not being compensated financially for the major changes in planning and staffing that the change in scope is creating. Moreover, you may find that the impact of the suggested move on the original objectives is very damaging.

FACTORS LEADING TO SCOPE CREEP

1 A fear of turning down a client or seeming to oppose the wishes of a senior director.

2 Underestimation of the financial and personal effect of changing a project plan.

3 Over-optimism on the new suggestion to improve a potentially difficult situation.

4 A lack of faith in the original project plan, which reflects badly on the process.

5 The technical team's desire to over-engineer a solution and to inject its own creative take on the original plan.

HOW TO CONTROL SCOPE CREEP

1 Go back to your original plan and to the reasons for launching the project in the first place. If you believe in the logic of the first plan, the reasons for shifting the parameters are going to have to be very convincing.

2 Think through the consequences of not making the change and be honest about the repercussions of 'doing nothing'.

3 Don't be afraid to be honest with your client or overall boss and explain why the proposed changes could hinder the project.

Managing risk

Given that projects are often conceived as bold attempts to instigate change, they are by nature risky ventures. The fact that the final result is uncertain doesn't mean, however, that you can't do your best to identify potential risks, to assess their potential effect on the project and to devise strategies to minimize their negative impact. These are some steps to take to become effective at dealing with uncertainty.

1 IDENTIFY RISKS

It's no use burying your head in the sand. Every project has certain sources of risk, such as product risk, where the product risks not living up to expectation; schedule risk, where tasks using new technology run the danger of taking longer than you have time for; and resource risks, where your existing facilities, equipment and staff are not capable of meeting the project's requirements.

2 DEAL WITH RISKS

Once you've identified the exact nature of the risk, you can turn to experts or consultants who understand more about the unknown product or service or you can look at other companies that have embarked on a similar venture. It is possible to learn from other companies' successes as well as their failures.

3 ESTIMATE THE FUTURE

Don't be content with simply stating that 'the project is risky'. Explain in what ways the project presents future risks, and calculate exactly how likely it is that the risks will actually occur. Seek out examples of other projects with similar ambitions, and ask expert opinions.

4 BE OBJECTIVE

By the time you've worked out some probabilities and specified the nature of the risks, you might conclude that the worst possible scenario for the project is rather distant.

5 DEVELOP RISK-MANAGEMENT STRATEGY
Once you've decided that you can, to some extent, decide which risks are acceptable to you and the project, then you can develop contingency plans in case the worst-case scenario does occur. This might mean having a 'plan B' when your first course of action fails.

6 COMMUNICATE RISKS
The more people with whom you share your concern about risk factors, the more feedback you can hope to receive on the perceived risks and the more confidence you will acquire to handle them, whether by devising alternative strategies or by garnering future support.

Project management software

Computer software is a popular tool in project management. A list of the main benefits of software follows.

1 EASIER STORAGE/RETRIEVAL OF INFORMATION
The constant and easy access to information is so important when you are managing a project that any software that improves your existing methods of storing and sharing information will prove to be a major asset to your operation.

2 ANALYZING INFORMATION
As there are invariably many changes to a project plan once activities are underway, it's important to take a flexible approach to shifting circumstances. The ability to analyze and update information is a further advantage of using management software.

3 PREPARING REPORTS AND PRESENTATIONS
Another aspect of effective communication during a project
is frequent updates and presentations to staff and clients.
Software that can help to present any ongoing results in a
professional format will improve your communication channel
and will make stakeholders feel that they are 'in the loop' at
all stages.

Most of the disadvantages of relying on software are not so much the fault of the actual technology but of the user's attitude towards the software. Below are some problems to avoid.

1

INACCURATE DATA
There is a temptation to become careless about entering information into a system when users put too much faith in the software to sort any potential mistakes or inaccuracies out. Excellent software cannot make up for poor research or missing information.

2

LACK OF RESPONSIBILITY
An over-reliance on software to spot mistakes or to create impressive-looking documents can encourage users to postpone difficult decisions by failing to stand back and look at the bigger picture.

3 LOSS OF TEAM COMMUNICATION/SPIRIT
When users of software get too involved with the intricacies
of reports, data and graphs and stop discussing issues with
colleagues or clients, some team members can become
isolated and fail to pass on important information.

Dedicated software

FEATURES

Dedicated software is stand-alone, separate software packages that are used for specific areas of your project. Some examples are:

1 SPREADSHEETS: Microsoft Excel is one of the most popular packages for making repetitive calculations.

2 WORD PROCESSING: Microsoft Word is among the leading programs for written communications and progress reports.

3 CALENDAR: A well-known package for address books and to-do lists is Microsoft Outlook.

4 DATABASE: Microsoft Access is commonly used for the storage and retrieval of large chunks of data.

5 BUSINESS PRESENTATION: Most managers are expected to be able to use PowerPoint to prepare overheads and slide shows.

ADVANTAGES

1 Most computers today have one or more elements of these packages already available so they are accessible and well known.

2 It's easy to measure the efficiency of packages that focus on no more than two functions.

DISADVANTAGES

1 It's not always possible to integrate information easily on one package (for instance, a spreadsheet) with that on a different package (a day planner, for example).

2 When you are looking at separate elements of a project in different packages, you may lose sight of the bigger picture.

Integrated software

FEATURES

As its name suggests, integrated software combines most of the features available in stand-alone, dedicated software. These are some of the most common capabilities of integrated software.

1 Calculate project budget.

2 Monitor scheduled start and end dates for activities.

3 Present schedule in Gantt chart and table formats.

4 Create list of all activities and their components.

5 Build schedules that include task durations and interdependencies between tasks.

6 Assess the impact of schedule and resources on overall project plan.

7 Designate team members to specific tasks.

ADVANTAGES

1 Packages have a choice of preprogrammed report formats to use in presentations or to update reports.

2 The separate functions of the package are linked so data is only entered once.

DISADVANTAGES

1 Users must understand and receive training on all the functions of the package to appreciate all the software's capabilities. In addition, many would-be users are put off by the high costs involved in buying integrated packages.

Checklist: project management software

1 Do you understand the principles of project management and are you seeking software to enhance your operation rather than to make up for any uncertainties you have with the project? ☐

2 Have you asked the company or team members what software, if any, has been used before? If the company has experience with the software, what were the past benefits and disadvantages of the package? ☐

3 Do you have evidence that the software you are looking at has been successfully used in other companies involved in similar projects? Is it relevant to your company experience? ☐

4 Have you considered a formal training programme on the software package? Will it save you time and money in the long run?

☐

5 Does the budget allow for investment in new technology? Do you really need the software? Do the pros greatly outweigh the costs?

☐

CHECKLIST

Relaunching the project

The idea of revamping a project that appears to be failing is too depressing for many project managers, but there is nothing worse than sticking stubbornly to a plan just for the sake of it. Sometimes what appears to need a major overhaul might only need a few changes at different stages of the project. The following are some steps that can be used to help you to revive a flagging project.

1 UNDERSTAND THE PROBLEM
As argued in Chapter 1, pp. 10–45, defining a problem is halfway to resolving it. Try to describe exactly what has gone wrong with the project – for instance: 'It's running behind' or 'We've spent too much money' – and then try to explain why you're in this situation. For instance, you might reply with: 'People who were enthusiastic about the project have now moved on to other projects'.

2 SEEK MAIN BENEFICIARIES
When things seem to be going wrong, try to remember the end users who were urging this project along and what they stand to benefit. After you remind yourself of the potential advantages, you can inspire yourself to push ahead.

3 RESTATE PROJECT OBJECTIVES
Spell out the project objectives with the key backers of the project, even if it's as simple as 'to diversify into new markets'.

4 FOCUS ON ACTIVITIES
Having clearly established the objectives, turn to the activities or tasks that need to be completed to help you to achieve all your objectives.

5 RE-ENERGIZE THE TEAM
Now that you know what tasks need to be done, search for the team members who must direct these tasks and urge them to complete them by a realistic date.

6 REVISE THE TIMETABLE
With the team now ready to re-engage in the project's activities, you can modify the original timetable and set new time targets.

7 REVISE STAFF
After you've set new deadlines, make sure that you have the right number of staff to help you meet them. This might be the ideal time for a general staff meeting that reinstalls the project in an official manner.

8 CONSIDER THE RISKS
Make sure that you've thought of all the potential risks, put them into context and made provisions to handle them.

9 FOCUS ON MONITORING
Now that the project is up and running, make sure that you keep a very close eye on performance by insisting on regular check-ups and update reports.

Checklist: project monitoring

1 Have you created easy-to-use forms that the staff can fill in on a weekly basis? ☐

2 How long do you take to look through forms and include them in your own weekly report? ☐

3 Do you know how many people read your weekly report? ☐

4 Have you set a system in place to encourage feedback? ☐

5 Does the staff have the opportunity to meet at least once a week? ☐

6 Do you make sure every individual participant contributes to the meeting? ☐

7 Do you follow up meetings with a written report? ☐

8 Do you know if your project is delayed and, if so, by how many days/weeks? ☐

CHECKLIST

9 Do you know the reasons for the delays? ☐

10 Do you know if you've spent more on the project than the allocated budget? ☐

11 Can you identify if there are any increases or decreases in your budget? ☐

12 How many changes have you made to the project in the last week or so? Were they all necessary? ☐

13 Are you afraid of offending your customers/sponsors? ☐

14 Can you identify the main risks to your project? ☐

15 Have you made any contingency plans to minimize risks? Are funds set aside for contingency plans? ☐

CHECKLIST

7

closing down the project

The project closure plan

After weeks, maybe months, on a project, it may be tempting to get impatient as the finishing line approaches and to hurry the final stages. It is also inevitable that some members lose a lot of the initial enthusiasm, or simply run out of time, as they move on to new projects.

Neglecting the closure of a project is a major error, and the process, in fact, demands as much care and attention to detail as the first stage of the project plan. The following points underline the reasons for focusing closely on the last stage of a project:

1 MEASURES PROJECT SUCCESS
Without a proper assessment of the project's outcomes, it is impossible to gauge how well the project was conceived in the first place. Was the project's main objective achieved?

2 SATISFIES THE TEAM
Without a formal wrap up, the members of a team, who may well be dispersing to other divisions or other companies, fail to experience the sense of achievement of a job satisfactorily finished.

3 PAVES THE WAY FOR FUTURE TEAMWORK
You may also want to work with some of the team members
in the future, and they will be far more willing to work with
you if they think their efforts were recognized and they
garnered positive results.

4 AVOIDS REPEATING MISTAKES
If the team disbands and no proper records have been
completed and nobody is left to answer last-minute queries,
the chances of writing up a comprehensive final report are
much slimmer. The company will also fail to benefit from the
mistakes and insights made during this project. How much
easier would the project have been for you if you had been
able to refer to a previous project report?

5 CONTROLS EXPENSES

It is typical for people to formally end contracts with any suppliers of equipment or services that have been hired during the project. Bills may continue to arrive after the project has ended for services that are no longer required. This is unnecessarily wasteful.

6 PREVENTS PREMATURE DEPARTURES

If no formal closing-down activities have been planned, some team members may move to other projects before they have finished their tasks. This puts an added burden on those who are left behind – motivation will wane, further delaying the closing down process.

7 IMPROVES COMMUNICATION WITH END USERS
Whether the beneficiaries of the project are stakeholders,
customers or suppliers, the company will look far more
impressive if a report is sent to all the end users.

8 OFFERS PERSONAL SATISFACTION
The project you have overseen should be successful, and it
should be satisfying, from both a professional and personal
view, to have a written record of the challenges you faced and
how you overcame them to achieve success.

Tips for effective close-down

1 PLAN PROJECT TERMINATION
Ideally, a plan for close-down is already available in the plan
you drew up before the launch of the project. If you didn't plan
the termination stage, start thinking about it a few weeks
before the event, paying the same attention to time and
resources that you did for the project as a whole. Specify the
objectives, and measure whether these were met.

2 OBTAIN OFFICIAL APPROVAL
In the same way that you needed final approval for the launch
of the project, make sure that senior management, sponsors
or customers provide an official stamp of approval on the
project's results. Then you can confidently tell the team that
the project has come to a formal end.

3 CLOSE CHARGE ACCOUNTS
Any standing charges with suppliers of products, equipment or services, including basic items such as extra mobile phones, newspapers, food and drink should be settled and closed down to avoid unnecessary costs.

4 GATHER INFORMATION
Before the team members disappear, try to hold as many conversations and interviews as possible to find out what has been achieved and what is still pending in individual projects.

5 HELP TEAM WIND DOWN
The project manager often gets highly involved in the integration process of the team at the beginning of a project, when tensions are high and people are jockeying for position and grappling with diverse work patterns. Less attention is paid to the closing-down period, but members still need guidance from you. Start off by showing your appreciation for the work done, both in public – perhaps during a celebration – and also privately. It is even advisable to follow up with some brief comments in writing.

6 BE THERE RIGHT TO THE END
Also be accessible to the team in the final stages when some members may have left early and others are left with too many responsibilities. You need to avoid allowing the team to feel abandoned.

7 MONITOR RIGHT TO THE END
On the other hand, you need to make sure that team members understand that they can't move on to new work without having formally shown you that they have reached their targets.

8 HOLD A PROJECT REVIEW MEETING
Recapping all the key components of the project and assessing what worked and what didn't is essential to effective project management (see next page).

Project review meeting

A post-project review or evaluation meeting is an ideal opportunity to answer key questions about objectives and targets. These are recommended steps to follow.

COLLECT THE FOLLOWING INFORMATION

1 The pre-project scenario, a statement about the proposed changes and the outcome.

2 Total expenditure.

3 Total investment.

4 Unexpected changes to the project plan.

5 Response to project results by end users (sponsor, senior management, customers).

INFORMATION SOURCES

1 Interviews with key personnel.

2 Progress reports made during project.

3 Correspondence and e-mails during the project.

SEND INVITES TO A MEETING

Make sure all key players are able to attend a meeting. Hold the meeting away from the office if possible because a neutral environment may encourage team members to express their opinions. Mention that you will be looking at several aspects of the project, including the project plan, their own performance and that of colleagues. Let attendees know that the meeting is specifically to learn from achievements and mistakes rather than to point blame and air grievances with other people.

PLAN THE MEETING

A formal agenda during the meeting will ensure that all points are covered. Start off with an overall conclusion of the project's achievements and then go through the various stages of the project chronologically, putting a special emphasis on milestones where interim results can be best discussed. It is essential that you appoint a person to take down the minutes of the meeting so that a written summary of the points discussed can be sent to all attendees later.

QUESTIONS/ISSUES TO DISCUSS DURING THE MEETING

1 Did the project meet all its objectives?

2 For the objectives met, what aided success?

3 If some targets weren't met, what were the reasons? Was it because of unforeseen circumstances or lack of experience?

4 Was the project completed on time? If not, why not? Was this because of unrealistic expectations?

5 Was the project finished to budget? If not, what proved to be more expensive than planned? Were there costs that, in hindsight, could have been spared?

6 Were the milestones set to check on progress adequate indicators to measure progress? Were other methods used to monitor developments?

7 Were the proper number of people employed for the different tasks? Were any areas over- or understaffed?

8 When problems did emerge, were project directors or managers quick to respond?

9 What kind of feedback did you get from the end users?

10 What are the two main areas that could have been improved during the project?

11 Will a follow-up project be necessary?

12 What have you learned about the company during the project experience?

Close-down report

After the meeting and following an analysis of the findings, it is time to prepare a close-down report. Broadly, the report should indicate what practices were particularly successful and how they should be encouraged in the future, as well as what practices failed to achieve results and how they should be avoided. The following areas should be included:

1

OVERALL PERFORMANCE
The report should include a brief statement of the project's main goals and whether they were met. There should be details of what changes were implemented and why some targets weren't met.

2

USE OF RESOURCES
The report has to grade the availability and use of the main resources used in the project, mainly money and staff. Was funding inadequate or could savings have been made? Were there enough staff members? Did participants fulfil their roles adequately?

3 TIMING
The report should make it clear whether the allocated time scheduled for the project was realistic and in what ways the result would have been different if the work had started earlier or later.

4 PLUS/MINUS INDICATORS
There should be a list of strengths and weaknesses of the project that will help you and future readers of the report to analyze quickly and succinctly whether, in general, the project met its targets.

5 GREATEST SUCCESS/WEAKNESS
If you want your project to be used as a template or valuable reference point for future projects, highlighting some of the greatest highs and lows can act as incentives for future project managers.

Checklist: close-down

1 Have you informed all members of the team about the approximate date(s) for the closing down of the project? ☐

2 Have you set realistic enough targets to help you decide whether actions have helped to achieve the desired results? ☐

3 Have you sought approval from end users of the project? Are they satisfied with the completed work? ☐

4 Have you asked for feedback from a wide range of sources? ☐

5 Have you tracked down all the service and product providers and closed down their services to you? ☐

6 Have all suppliers, clients and staff been paid? ☐

7 Have you obtained all the necessary information about results and budgets? ☐

8 Have you made sure that the opinions of a wide range of people have been recorded? ☐

9 Have you compiled all your findings into a well-presented report? Have you sent the report out to all interested parties? ☐

10 Have you held a final meeting with all your key players? Did the meeting help to smooth some of the inevitable tensions that came up during the process? ☐

CHECKLIST

Celebrating and thanking

Keep the close-down phase of the project as upbeat as possible. This is doubly important if you are letting staff go rather than simply redeploying them for work on a new team.

CELEBRATING SUCCESS:

1 Fosters a spirit of collaboration

2 Improves morale

3 Underlines core values

HOW TO CELEBRATE:

1 Organize a gathering to celebrate the team's successes. If your organization regularly schedules social events, be sure that the purpose of this gathering is well disseminated.

2 Thank team members individually, if at all possible. If there are too many of them, make sure that you thank leaders and supervisors and that your thanks are passed on. Alternatively, send an e-mail to all team members, thanking them for their individual contributions.

3 If appropriate, ensure any bonuses for early delivery or outstripping targets are distributed in an equitable fashion.

4 Make sure team members who are leaving the organization know who to approach for references. Make sure human resources records are updated.

5 Post vacancy notices in other departments or at other sites.

6 Organize timely and tidy departures: It is demoralizing for staff who are leaving and staying to have individuals who are no longer contributing occupying office space. This is also not cost-effective.

Conclusion

This is a summary of the seven main stages that you will normally go through when managing a project.

1 DEFINE THE PROJECT

Give yourself ample time to define the main objectives of the project. After you've pinned down the project vision, check with key players and sponsors that they agree with the project definition. Also identify any potential obstacles and know that you can overcome them. You need to be convinced that the project is viable.

2 PLAN THE PROJECT

To help you create a plan, you need to draw up a list of all the activities necessary to move your objectives forward. You will also have to devise a way of monitoring these tasks such as setting milestones during the project that will indicate that the activities have achieved results.

3 ESTIMATE TIME, MONEY AND RESOURCES
You're now entering the nitty-gritty stage of planning. Three key questions need to be answered: how much time will the project take? What resources does the project need? How much will the project cost? Make sure senior management approves these estimates.

4 BUILD A PROJECT TEAM
When you build a team, make sure that each member fills a functional and technical role and that they understand their tasks. Also try to mix different personalities that will complement each other.

5 LAUNCH THE PROJECT
Before the project launch, try to identify all the possible risks
so that you're ready to combat them if necessary. You're now
ready for the start-up report that summarizes the project's
objectives, constraints and targets. After the formal launch,
time pressures will intensify, so an effective communication
system and immediate access to information will help a
project to flow easily and swiftly.

6 MONITOR THE PROJECT
One of the most common ways of keeping track of different
activities and resolving any inevitable hiccups is to produce a
written weekly report. You also need to arrange review
meetings where participants can air their views openly. Be
ready for last-minute tweaks to your plan. This is the norm. Be
alert to clients introducing new parameters in the final stages
of the project. If there are dramatic changes, make sure you
inform everyone.

7 CLOSE DOWN THE PROJECT
It's easy to neglect the closure of a project, but closing down deserves meticulous planning. As you approach the finishing line, try to measure whether you've met your objectives. If you have, obtain a stamp of approval from senior management or customers. A project review meeting is an ideal opportunity to answer key questions about objectives and targets. Finally, follow this up with a close-down report that confirms achievements in writing.

Index